# Contents

Words in **bold** can be found in the glossary.

Cities everywhere

Cities are large settlements where thousands, and sometimes millions, of people live and work. Many British cities developed around a cathedral or a castle, built hundreds of years ago.

Some cities near the sea became busy ports, where ships loaded and unloaded goods. **Industrial** cities grew around factories.

▲ The city of Winchester grew in medieval times. Huge numbers of **pilgrims** came to visit its cathedral.

▼ Liverpool, on the north-west coast, was once England's main **transatlantic** port. It had seven miles of **docks**.

Look around you
City

Ruth Thomson

Photography by Chris Fairclough

WAYLAND

First published in 2007 by Wayland

Reprinted in 2008 by Wayland

This paperback edition published in 2010 by Wayland

Wayland
338 Euston Road
London NW1 3BH

Wayland Australia
Level 17/207 Kent Street
Sydney, NSW 2000

Editor: Victoria Brooker
Designer: Elaine Wilkinson
Concept design: Paul Cherrill

The author and publisher would like the thank the following: H.R. Thompson; for use of photographs in this book: page 4 (top) Roy Rainford/Robert Harding World Imagery/Corbis; page 5 Andy Hibbert/Collections Picture Library; page 9 Skyscan/Corbis.

British Library Cataloguing in Publication Data

Thomson, Ruth
In a city. – (Look around you)
    1. Cities and towns – Juvenile literature 2. City and town life –
    Juvenile literature 3. Human ecology – Juvenile literature
    I. Title
    910.9'1732
ISBN 978 0 7502 6177 7

Printed in China

Wayland is a division of Hachette Children's Books, an Hachette UK Company
www.hachette.co.uk

Edinburgh, the **capital** of Scotland, surrounds an ancient castle built on the top of a rocky hill.

Leeds became an industrial city in Victorian times. Rows of houses were built for workers near cotton mills and factories.

City features

Cities are busy places, full of shops, offices and places to eat and drink. Most have an indoor or outdoor market.

There are also places where people can relax, such as parks, gardens and sports centres.

▲ A river often runs through the centre of a city. The river Thames runs through London.

▼ Every day, thousands of peop go shopping in city centres.

LOOK CLOSER!

What features do you notice in a city park?

◀ Covered shopping centres attract shoppers in bad weather.

▼ Indoor markets, such as this one in Leeds, sell fruit, flowers, fish, cheese and vegetables.

City buildings

◀ This big Town Hall is in Manchester

Cities have many large, grand buildings, such as a Town Hall, concert halls, theatres, museums and art galleries.

Most cities have a university. Every city has one or more football clubs.

▼ At night, city centres are brightly lit as people come to visit the theatre, the cinema or to eat out.

◀ Some cities have built new buildings, like this one in Glasgow. This is a place for meetings and exhibitions.

Museums often ve collections of , nature, science costume. Some ve displays about e local area.

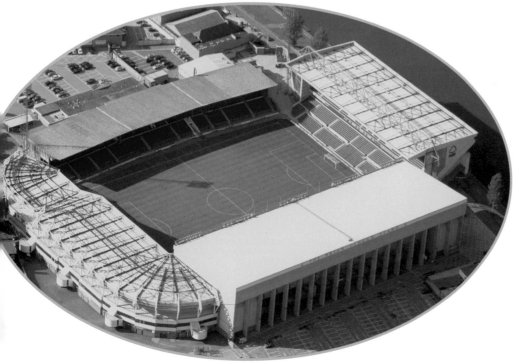

◀ Each football club has its own ground, where home matches are played.

Homes

Near city centres, many old houses line the streets joined together in rows, called terraces. Big houses are often divided into flats. When old houses are knocked down, they are often replaced by high-rise flats.

In the **suburbs**, where there is much more space, houses are often **semi-detached** or **detached**.

▲ High-rise blocks of flats

▲ Terraced houses usually have small gardens or yards.

Roads in the suburbs are quiet and sometimes lined with trees. Houses have a garden and, often, a garage too.

New flats are being built in city centres for people who want to live close to where they work.

LOOK CLOSER!

What might be good about living in a city centre or the suburbs? What might be bad?

Work

More people work in cities than live in them. Many workers make long journeys to work every day. These people are called commuters.

There is a huge variety of jobs in cities. People work in offices, shops, hotels, hospitals, supermarkets or cafes. They drive delivery vans, buses or taxis. They collect rubbish, mend roads and construct new buildings.

▲ Crowds of commuters trav to work and back by train.

▼ There is a wide choice of food shops in cities.

▲ Some people work outdoors, helping to keep cities clean and pleasant.

◀ The police help to keep city streets safe.

LOOK CLOSER!

What other jobs might you
see people doing on city streets?

Signs of the past

Most cities have a long history. Some were once walled. Remains of their walls and gates may still be seen.

Statues, memorials and **plaques** may tell you who once lived in a city. Street names give clues about what took place there in the past. Old buildings may still stand, although their use has often changed.

▲ In the past, city gates were closed at night

► Cities often put up statues to celebrate important people.

◄ War memorials list the names of people who died fighting in World War I and II.

◀ Large public clocks were useful when watches were not common.

▶ Fountains once provided clean drinking water for people who did not have running water at home.

◀ Many northern towns have old factory buildings, which have now become museums, offices or homes.

LOOK CLOSER!

Find street names that tell you who once worked there or that recall a market, an entertainment or a punishment.

CANDLEMAKER ROW

WEST PARLIAMENT SQUARE

LAWNMARKET

BAKERS ALLEY

Moving around

Motorways and fast, frequent train services link most cities. The biggest cities have airports, as well.

City streets are full of traffic. People are being persuaded to walk or cycle, or to use buses, trains or trams instead of cars.

▲ Motorways are used for transporting goods, as well as people.

▼ City centre streets are usually crowded with cars, delivery vans, buses and taxis.

▲ London has an underground railway, known as the tube.

▲ A network of railways link major cities across Britain.

▶ This free bus encourages people to use public transport.

◀ Taxis are useful for visitors and people with luggage.

London

London is the **capital** of England and the biggest city in Great Britain. It is home to seven million people, many from countries all over the world.

London is a centre for banking, business and law. Millions of tourists visit the city every year to see its famous sights.

▲ Members of Parliament (MPs) sit in the Houses of Parliament to discuss and make new **laws**.

▼ Buckingham Palace is the home of Queen Elizabeth II. It has 600 rooms and a large garden.

▲ The Tower of London is more than 900 year old. It houses the Crown Jewels and a large collection of weapons and armour.

▲ From the top of the London Eye, on the bank of the River Thames, you can see most London sights.

▲ Covent Garden was once a fruit, flower and vegetable market. It is now filled with shops, and stalls selling arts and crafts.

▲ Thousands of people work in office blocks at Canary Wharf.

Mapping a city

Look closely at the map. Notice how:

- the city has built up around the cathedral
- the railway and bus stations are both near the city centre
- the city has parks for people to use

▶ Railway station

▼ Bus station

▶ Cathedral

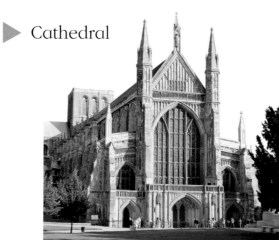

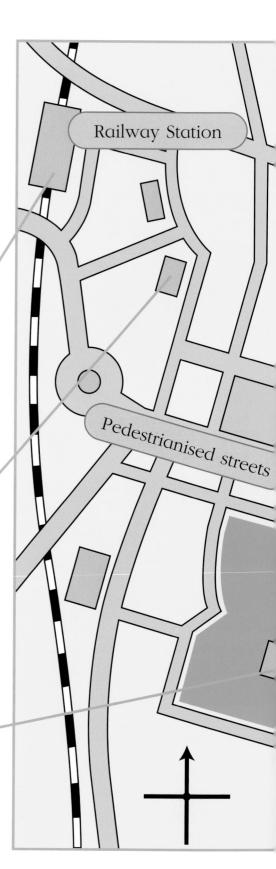

Railway Station

Pedestrianised streets

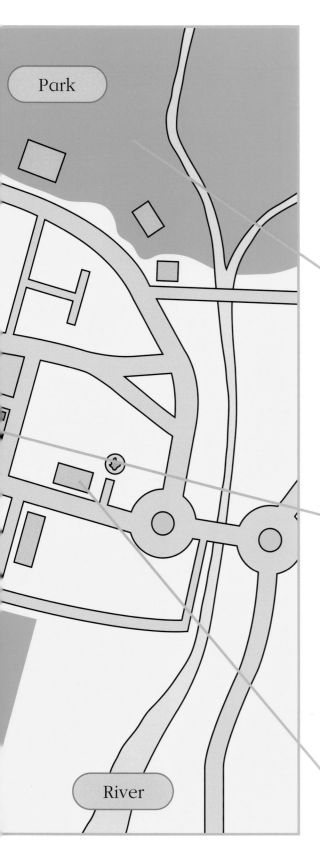

Park

River

Make a map of a city centre.

- Mark where important buildings are, such as a cathedral, town hall, theatre or museum.
- Mark the railway and bus stations.
- Mark the main shopping area and the market.
- Put in any parks, squares or other green areas.

▲ Park

▲ Market

▼ Museum

A walk in a city

Take a walk around a city centre and see how many different signs you can spot.

- Some signs direct **pedestrians** to sights and services.
- Road signs tell drivers which way to go and where to park.
- Maps help visitors find their way from one place to another.

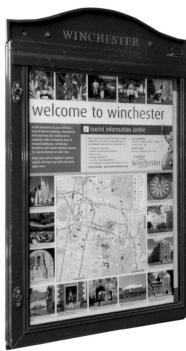

City map

▼ ▶ Road signs for drivers

PEDESTRIAN ZONE

No vehicles

Mon - Sat
11 am - 3 pm

At any time

▼ ▶ Information signs for pedestrians

ake a list or take
hotographs of
ings that help
ake a city a
easant place to be.
ere are some ideas
 get you started.

Places to sit

Green spaces – parks, gardens or squares

Street entertainers

Art and flower displays

Traffic free, well-lit streets,
which are safe for pedestrians

Glossary

MALPAS

7/7/18

capital the most important city of a country

detached a detached house stands on its own

docks the part of a harbour where ships load and unload their goods

industrial relating to factories and making products

laws the rules for everyone who live in a country

pedestrian someone who walks on pavements or roads

pilgrim someone who makes a journey to a holy place

plaque a metal plate with writing on it about a famous person or event, usually fixed to a building

semi-detached a semi-detached house is joined to another house on one side

suburb an area of houses on the edge of a town or city

transatlantic crossing the Atlantic Ocean – for example from England to the USA

 # Index